ℰꙨ

# This Journal Belongs To

_____

Date _____

❦

## Brownlow Personal Reflections Collection

And Serve It with Love Recipe Collector
Leaves of Gold Daily Planner
Family & Friends Address Book
For All My Special Days Birthday Book
God's Promises for Every Day Journal
Refresh My Heart Prayer Journal
Perpetual Calenders
Write Ideas Blank Journals

*Those who hope in the Lord will renew their strength.*
*They will soar on wings like eagles;*
*they will run and not grow weary, they will walk*
*and not be faint.*

**ISAIAH 40:31**

꽃잎

You will find, as you look back upon your life,
that the moments when you really lived
are the moments when you have done things
in the spirit of love.

HENRY DRUMMOND

ईश

*What, then, shall we say in response to this?*
*If God is for us, who can be against us?*

**ROMANS 8:31**

Life's greatest tragedy is to lose God and not to miss Him.

F. W. NORWOOD

*The Lord has done great things for us,*
*and we are filled with joy.*

**PSALM 126:3**

&

_____

_____

_____

_____

_____

_____

_____

_____

_____

_____

_____

_____

_____

_____

_____

_____

_____

_____

_____

_____

_____

_____

_____

_____

_____

*Be a life long or short, its completeness*
*depends on what it was lived for.*

DAVID STARR JORDAN

*So we fix our eyes not on what is seen,
but on what is unseen. For what is seen is temporary,
but what is unseen is eternal.*

**2 CORINTHIANS 4:18**

*The only ones among you who will be really happy are those who will have sought and found how to serve.*

ALBERT SCHWEITZER

❦

*The grass withers and the flowers fall,*
*but the word of our God stands forever.*

**Isaiah 40:8**

_____
_____
_____
_____
_____
_____
_____
_____
_____
_____
_____
_____
_____
_____
_____
_____
_____
_____
_____
_____
_____
_____
_____
_____
_____
_____

ها

ૐ

*Let us not go faster than God. It is our emptiness
and our thirst that he needs, not our plentitude.*

JACQUES MARITAIN

ૐ

*In God I trust; I will not be afraid.*
*What can man do to me?*

**PSALM 56:11**

*Wherever there is a human being,*
*there is an opportunity for kindness.*

SENECA

*But thanks be to God! He gives us the victory through our Lord Jesus Christ.*

**1 CORINTHIANS 15:57**

Were there no God we would be in this glorious world
with grateful hearts and no one to thank.

CHRISTINA ROSSETTI

*I have come into the world as a light, so that no one who believes in me should stay in darkness.*

JOHN 12:46

*Worry does not empty tomorrow of its sorrow;*
*it empties today of its strength.*

CORRIE TEN BOOM

৪৩

*The Lord does not look at the things man looks at.*
*Man looks at the outward appearance,*
*but the Lord looks at the heart.*

**1 SAMUEL 16:7**

৪৯

ৎ৯

৭৩

§

Those who would have nothing to do with thorns
must never attempt to gather flowers.

૬૭

*The Lord himself goes before you and will be with you; he will never leave you nor forsake you. Do not be afraid; do not be discouraged.*

**DEUTERONOMY 31:8**

*We have a God who delights in impossibilities.*

ANDREW MURRAY

৪২

*I love the Lord, for he heard my voice; he heard my cry*
*for mercy. Because he turned his ear to me,*
*I will call on him as long as I live.*

**PSALM 116:1,2**

*No one has the right to look with contempt on himself*
*when God has shown such an interest in him.*

*Your Father knows what you need before you ask him.*

MATTHEW 6:8

૪૭

*Handle them carefully, for words
have more power than atom bombs.*

PEARL STRACHAN

*And we know that in all things
God works for the good of those who love him.*

**ROMANS 8:28**

_____

_____

_____

_____

_____

_____

_____

_____

_____

_____

_____

_____

_____

_____

_____

_____

_____

_____

_____

_____

_____

_____

_____

_____

_____

_____

_____

*God nowhere tells us to give up things for the sake
of giving them up. He tells us to give them up for the sake
of the only thing worth having—life with Himself.*

OSWALD CHAMBERS

❦

*And my God will meet all your needs*
*according to his glorious riches in Christ Jesus.*

**PHILIPPIANS 4:19**

Do not have your concert first and tune your instruments afterward. Begin the day with God.

JAMES HUDSON TAYLOR

৪৩

*How great is the love the Father has lavished on us,*
*that we should be called children of God!*

**1 JOHN 3:1**

*What makes humility so desirable*
*is the marvelous thing it does to us; it creates in us*
*a capacity for the closest possible intimacy with God.*

MONICA BALDWIN

፠

*Do not be afraid, little flock, for your Father has been
pleased to give you the kingdom.*

LUKE 12:32

_____
_____
_____
_____
_____
_____
_____
_____
_____
_____
_____
_____
_____
_____
_____
_____
_____
_____
_____
_____
_____
_____
_____
_____
_____
_____

God loves us the way we are
but He loves us too much to leave us that way.

LEIGHTON FORD

*I will not forget you! See, I have engraved you*
*on the palms of my hands.*

ISAIAH 49:15,16

When we forget ourselves, we usually do something that everyone else remembers.

*I will put my law in their minds and write it on their hearts.*
*I will be their God and they will be my people.*

**JEREMIAH 31:33**

_____

_____

_____

_____

_____

_____

_____

_____

_____

_____

_____

_____

_____

_____

_____

_____

_____

_____

_____

_____

_____

_____

_____

_____

_____

_____

❧

Our love for God is tested
by whether we seek Him or His gifts.

RALPH SOCKMAN

*Above all else, guard your heart,*
*for it is the wellspring of life.*

**PROVERBS 4:23**

৪৩

※

*One of God's specialties is to make somebodies*
*out of nobodies.*

HENRIETTA MEARS

*He who has the Son has life; he who does not have the Son of God does not have life.*

1 JOHN 5:12